JORDAN LOOPMAN

Python Quick Reference Guide: The Cheat Sheet for Fast Learning

Learn Python's Key Concepts and Boost Your Coding Productivity

Contents

I Dedication

1 Chapter 1: Getting Started with Python 3

   Introduction to Python 4

   What is Python and Why Is It Popular? 5

   Overview of Python's Syntax and Design Philosophy 7

   Python vs. Other Programming Languages 9

   Setting Up Python 10

   Installing Python on Different Operating Systems 10

   Using Python's Interactive Shell (REPL) 14

   IDEs and Text Editors for Python Development 15

   You're Ready to Code! 17

   Running Your First Python Program 17

   1. Writing the "Hello, World!" Program 18

   2. Understanding Basic Syntax (Print Statements, Comments, etc.) 20

   3. Running Python Scripts from the Terminal 22

2 Chapter 2: Mastering Python Syntax and Basic Structures 25

   Variables and Data Types 26

   Defining Variables and Assigning Values 26

   Common Data Types: Strings, Integers, Floats, and Booleans 27

   Type Conversions and Type Checking 29

   Control Flow (Conditionals and Loops) in Python 30

   1. Using if, else, and elif Statements 31

   2. Writing for and while Loops 32

3. Understanding Loop Control Statements (break, continue)   34

Defining and Calling Functions   35

3   Chapter 3: Working with Python Libraries and Data Structures   38

Lists and Tuples in Python: Your Ultimate Guide to Data Management   39

Creating and Modifying Lists   39

Accessing Elements, Slicing, and Iterating Over Lists   41

Understanding Tuples and Their Immutability   42

Dictionaries and Sets: The Dynamic Duo of Data Storage   43

1. Using Dictionaries to Store Key-Value Pairs   44

2. Set Operations and Properties   45

3. Practical Examples of Dictionaries and Sets in Code   46

Using Built-in Libraries   48

Importing and Using Python's Standard Libraries   48

Practical Examples of os, random, and sys Libraries   49

Understanding the Importance of Python Packages   50

4   Chapter 4: Advanced Python Concepts and Productivity Tips   51

Working with Files   51

Reading from and Writing to Files   54

Error Handling and Debugging   58

5   Wrapping Up Your Python Journey   61

The Road You've Traveled   63

Why Python Matters   63

Where to Go Next?   64

Parting Words of Wisdom   65

6   References   67

7   About the Author: Jordan Loopman   68

II   A Small Request (But a Big Deal for Me!)

I

Dedication

To the curious minds who dare to learn,
To the late-night coders fueled by caffeine and sheer willpower,
To the bug hunters who whisper, "Why won't you work?" at 3 AM,
And to the future tech wizards who will one day automate their
own coffee machines—

This book is for you.

May your syntax be flawless, your logic unbreakable, and your
debugging swift.
And if all else fails, just remember: turn it off and on again.

Keep coding, keep creating, and never stop debugging!

1

Chapter 1: Getting Started with Python

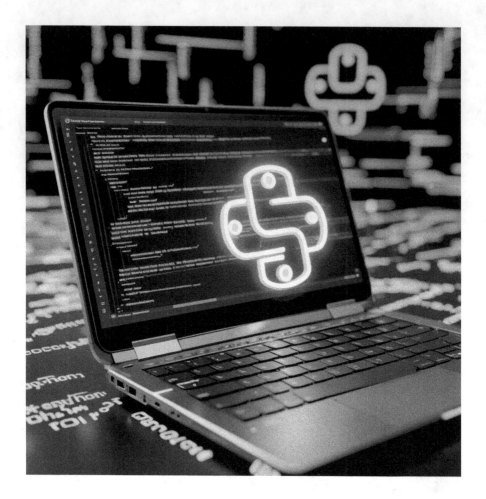

Introduction to Python

W elcome to the world of Python, where coding feels less like deciphering an alien language and more like having a friendly chat with your computer. If you've ever looked at complex programming languages and thought, *"There's got to be a simpler way,"* congratulations—you just described Python.

Python is the programming world's equivalent of a universal remote. It's powerful, easy to learn, and works across countless domains, from web development to artificial intelligence. But what exactly makes it so popular, and how does it compare to other languages? Buckle up, because we're about to take a deep dive into Python's greatness.

What is Python and Why Is It Popular?

The Short Answer:

Python is a high-level, interpreted programming language known for its simplicity, readability, and vast ecosystem. It's beginner-friendly, yet powerful enough for experts to use in cutting-edge fields like AI, data science, and automation.

The Long Answer (With More Flair):

Python was created in 1991 by Guido van Rossum, a programmer who must have thought, *"What if programming didn't have to feel like solving a 1,000-piece puzzle in the dark?"* His solution was Python—a language designed to be as human-friendly as possible.

Here's why Python has become a superstar in the programming world:

1. It Reads Like English (Almost)

Take a look at this Python code:

```
if temperature > 30:
    print("It's hot outside!")
```

Even if you've never written a line of code in your life, you can probably guess what this does. Now compare that to a similar condition in C++:

```
if (temperature > 30) {
std::cout « "It's hot outside!" « std::endl;
```

}

See the difference? Python eliminates unnecessary symbols and keeps things clean and readable.

2. One Language, Many Uses

Python is like the duct tape of programming—it works for everything. Whether you're building a website, analyzing data, automating tasks, or training an AI model, Python has a library for you.

Where is Python used?

- **Web Development** – Django, Flask
- **Data Science & Machine Learning** – Pandas, NumPy, Scikit-Learn, TensorFlow
- **Automation & Scripting** – Writing scripts to automate repetitive tasks
- **Cybersecurity & Ethical Hacking** – Used for penetration testing tools
- **Game Development** – Pygame (Yes, people build games with Python!)

3. The Python Community is Huge

Programming alone can feel like trying to fix a car with no manual. Fortunately, Python has one of the largest and most active communities in the world. Stuck on a problem? Chances are, someone else has already solved it and posted the answer on Stack Overflow.

4. It's the Darling of Big Companies

You know Python is a big deal when companies like Google, Netflix, NASA, and Facebook are using it. Want to analyze massive datasets like Netflix does? Python. Want to automate tasks like NASA's space missions? Python.

Even Instagram runs on Python. So the next time you scroll through memes for an hour, you can thank Python for making that possible.

Overview of Python's Syntax and Design Philosophy

Python was built with one core philosophy: **Keep It Simple, Stupid (KISS).**

This philosophy is formalized in something called *The Zen of Python*, a collection of guiding principles for writing Pythonic code. You can read them yourself by typing this in the Python terminal:

import this

You'll see gems of wisdom like:

- *"Beautiful is better than ugly."*
- *"Simple is better than complex."*
- *"Readability counts."*

1. Python's Clean Syntax

Python ditches the brackets and semicolons that clutter other languages.

Example in Python:

```
def greet(name):
print(f"Hello, {name}!")
```

Now compare that to Java:

```
public class Main {
public static void greet(String name) {
System.out.println("Hello, " + name + "!");
}
}
```

Python wins in readability every time.

2. Whitespace and Indentation

Python uses indentation instead of curly braces {} to define blocks of code.
Python:
```
if is_hungry:
print("Time to eat!")
```

C++:
```
if (is_hungry) {
std::cout « "Time to eat!";
}
```

Some programmers coming from other languages complain about this at first, but trust me—after a while, you'll wonder why all languages don't do this.

3. Dynamic Typing

Unlike Java or C++, you don't have to specify data types when declaring variables. Python figures it out for you.
Python:
```
x = 10 # No need to declare x as an integer
y = "Hello" # Python knows y is a string
```

C++:
```
int x = 10;
std::string y = "Hello";
```

Less code, fewer headaches.

Python vs. Other Programming Languages

Python is fantastic, but how does it stack up against other big players in the programming world? Let's do a quick comparison.

1. Python vs. Java

Java is great for large-scale applications, but Python wins for beginners and fast development.

2. Python vs. C++

C++ is powerful but complex, whereas Python is easy and flexible.

3. Python vs. JavaScript

JavaScript dominates the web, but Python rules everywhere else.

Python isn't just a language—it's an experience. It's simple, elegant, and powerful. Whether you're automating boring tasks, analyzing data, or building the next big app, Python makes it possible without breaking your brain.

If programming languages were superheroes, Python would be Batman—versatile, resourceful, and always ready for the job.

So if you're wondering whether you should learn Python, the answer is a resounding **YES.** Python isn't just a skill—it's a superpower. And now that you've had your first taste of Python's awesomeness, it's time to dive even deeper.

Setting Up Python

So, you've decided to take the plunge into Python. Congratulations! You're about to install one of the most versatile and beginner-friendly programming languages on the planet. But before you start writing code that automates your coffee maker or predicts the stock market (good luck with that), you need to set up Python on your machine properly.

This Section will guide you through installing Python on different operating systems, using the interactive shell (also known as the REPL), and choosing the right IDE or text editor for your coding adventures.

By the end of this section, you'll be fully equipped to write Python code like a pro—or at least like someone who knows where their Python interpreter is located.

Installing Python on Different Operating Systems

Before you can write Python code, you need Python itself. Thankfully, Python is available for all major operating systems, and installing it is as painless as ordering takeout (assuming you don't live in an area where food delivery is an urban legend).

Step 1: Checking if Python is Already Installed

Believe it or not, Python might already be on your system. To check, open your terminal or command prompt and type:

On Windows:

python —version

or
```
python3 —version
```

On macOS and Linux:

python3 —version

If you see something like this:
  Python 3.10.6

Congratulations! Python is already installed. Skip to the next section.
  If you see something like:
  'python' is not recognized as an internal or external command...

or
  Command not found

Then, my friend, you need to install Python. Let's do that now.

Installing Python on Windows

1. **Download Python:**

- Head over to Python's official website and download the latest version for Windows.
- Make sure you download the version labeled **Python 3.x.x** (not Python 2, which is older than your childhood memories).

1. **Run the Installer:**

- Double-click the .exe file you downloaded.
- Check the box that says **"Add Python to PATH"** (this is crucial—if you forget, you'll have to manually set it later, and nobody wants that).
- Click **Install Now** and wait for the magic to happen.

1. **Verify Installation:**

- Open Command Prompt (Win + R, then type cmd and hit Enter).

Type:
python —version

- If Python responds with its version number, you're good to go.

Installing Python on macOS

If you're using a Mac, Python 2 might be installed by default, but Python 2 is as outdated as flip phones. You need Python 3.

Method 1: Install via the Official Website

1. Go to Python's official downloads page.
2. Download the macOS installer.
3. Open the .pkg file and follow the installation instructions.

Verify by opening Terminal and running:
python3 —version

Method 2: Install via Homebrew (Recommended for Developers)

If you use Homebrew, installing Python is even easier.
Open Terminal and type:

1. brew install python
2. Wait for Homebrew to do its thing.

3. Verify installation with:

python3 —version

Installing Python on Linux

Good news, Linux users! Most Linux distributions come with Python pre-installed. However, it might be an older version, and you probably want the latest one.

To Install Python on Ubuntu/Debian-based distros:

sudo apt update
   sudo apt install python3

To Install Python on Fedora:

sudo dnf install python3

To Install Python on Arch Linux:

sudo pacman -S python

After installation, confirm that Python is installed by running:
   python3 —version

Using Python's Interactive Shell (REPL)

Alright, Python is installed! Now, let's talk about the **interactive shell**, also known as the REPL (Read-Eval-Print Loop).

What is REPL?

The REPL is like a chat window where you can type Python code and see instant results. It's perfect for testing small snippets of code without writing an entire script.

How to Open the Python Shell

Windows:

Open Command Prompt and type:
    python
    or
    python3

- **macOS/Linux:**

Open Terminal and type:
    python3
    You should see something like this:
    Python 3.x.x (default, Jul 10 2024, 14:20:28)
    [GCC 8.4.0] on linux
    Type "help", "copyright", "credits" or "license" for more information.
    »>

This means Python is ready to take commands.

Trying Out Some Python Code in REPL

Example 1: Simple Math

```
»> 5 + 3
  8
```

Example 2: Printing a Message

```
»> print("Hello, Python!")
  Hello, Python!
```

Example 3: Variables and Loops

```
»> x = 10
  »> for i in range(x):
  ... print(i)
  ...
```

Whenever you want to exit the REPL, just type:

```
  exit()
```

or press Ctrl + D.

IDEs and Text Editors for Python Development

Now that you can run Python, let's talk about where you should write your code. You have two main options:

- **Text Editors** (Lightweight, fast)

- **IDEs (Integrated Development Environments)** (Powerful, feature-rich)

Popular Text Editors

1. VS Code (Highly Recommended)

- Free, lightweight, and packed with extensions.
- Install Python extensions for auto-completion and debugging.
- Download here: https://code.visualstudio.com/.

2. Sublime Text

- Super fast and lightweight.
- Great for quick scripting.

3. Atom

- Developed by GitHub.
- Good for Python, but not as popular as VS Code.

Popular IDEs for Python

1. PyCharm (Best for Serious Development)

- Made for Python with top-notch debugging tools.
- Free community edition available.
- Download here: https://www.jetbrains.com/pycharm/.

2. Jupyter Notebook (Best for Data Science)

- Great for running code interactively, especially for data analysis.
- Install it with: pip install jupyter

3. IDLE (Comes with Python by Default)

- Simple, built-in editor.
- Good for beginners but lacks advanced features.

You're Ready to Code!

You've installed Python, learned how to use the interactive shell, and picked an IDE. You're now fully equipped to start writing Python scripts.

Running Your First Python Program

So, you've installed Python, set up your environment, and you're ready to write your first line of code. This is where the magic begins. If programming were a video game, this would be Level 1—the tutorial stage where you press a few buttons and get rewarded with instant gratification. Today, that reward is printing *Hello, World!* to your screen.

Why do programmers start with *Hello, World!*? Because it's simple, universal, and it confirms that everything is working. If you can print text to the screen, you're on your way to writing powerful Python applications. Now, let's dive in.

1. Writing the "Hello, World!" Program

The Birth of a Classic

The "Hello, World!" program has been a tradition since the dawn of programming. It started in the 1970s when Brian Kernighan, co-creator of the C programming language, used it in his book *The C Programming Language*. Since then, it has become the official handshake of programmers worldwide.

In Python, printing *Hello, World!* is as easy as breathing. Here's the code:
print("Hello, World!")

That's it. No semicolons, no curly braces, no compiling. Just one line of code. Beautiful, isn't it?

Step-by-Step Guide to Writing and Running Your First Program

Step 1: Open a Text Editor or IDE

You need a place to write your code. You can use:

- **A simple text editor** (Notepad, TextEdit, or Nano)
- **An IDE (Integrated Development Environment)** (VS Code, PyCharm, or IDLE)

For beginners, IDLE (which comes with Python) is a great choice.

Step 2: Write the Code

Open your editor and type:
print("Hello, World!")

This is a function call. The print() function is a built-in function that tells Python to display whatever is inside the parentheses. The text inside the quotes is called a **string**.

Step 3: Save the File

Save the file with a .py extension, which stands for Python. Name it hello.py.

Step 4: Run the Program

On Windows (Command Prompt or PowerShell):

1. Open Command Prompt (press Win + R, type cmd, and hit Enter).

Navigate to the folder where you saved your file:

cd path\to\your\file

1. Run the script:python hello.py

On macOS/Linux (Terminal):

1. Open Terminal.

Navigate to the directory where you saved your script:

cd path/to/your/file

1. Run the script:python3 hello.py

1. If everything is set up correctly, you should see this:

Hello, World!

Congratulations! You've just run your first Python program. Take a moment to celebrate.

2. Understanding Basic Syntax (Print Statements, Comments, etc.)

Now that you've seen Python in action, let's break down its syntax and key features.

The print() Function

The print() function is your best friend in Python. It helps you display output and debug code. You can print numbers, strings, or even multiple items at once:

```
print("Welcome to Python!")
print(42)
print("The answer is:", 42)
```

Output:

```
Welcome to Python!
42
The answer is: 42
```

Notice how the last print() combines text and a number. Python automatically adds a space between them.

Comments: Leaving Notes in Your Code

In programming, comments are notes that explain what your code does. Python ignores them when running your script.

Single-line Comments:

Use # to write a comment:
```
# This is a comment
print("Hello, World!") # This prints a message
```

Multi-line Comments:

Use triple quotes (""" or ''') to write multi-line comments:
```
"""
This is a multi-line comment.
Python will ignore this.
"""

print("Python is fun!")
```

Use comments to explain complex code. Your future self will thank you.

Variables: Storing Data

Variables store values so you can reuse them later:
```
name = "Alice"
age = 25
print(name, "is", age, "years old.")
```

Output:
```
Alice is 25 years old.
```

Python doesn't require you to declare variable types. It figures it out on its own.

Indentation: Python's Secret Sauce

Unlike other languages that use curly braces {} for blocks of code, Python relies on indentation (spaces or tabs):

```
if 10 > 5:
    print("10 is greater than 5") # Indented code belongs to the if statement
```

Indentation isn't optional—it's required. If you forget to indent properly, Python will throw an error.

3. Running Python Scripts from the Terminal

Now that you know the basics, let's explore different ways to run Python scripts.

Method 1: Running a Script from the Terminal

We already covered this earlier. Just navigate to your script's location and type:

```
python hello.py
```

or

```
python3 hello.py # For macOS/Linux
```

Method 2: Running Python Interactively

Python has an interactive mode where you can type commands directly into the interpreter. Open your terminal and type:

```
python
```

or

```
python3 # For macOS/Linux
```

You'll see something like this:

```
Python 3.x.x (default, YYYY-MM-DD, ...)
[GCC ...] on ...
Type "help", "copyright", "credits" or "license" for more information.
»>
```

Now you can type Python commands directly:

```
»> print("Hello, World!")
Hello, World!
»> 2 + 2
4
```

To exit, type:

```
»> exit()
```

Method 3: Running Python Scripts Inside an IDE

If you're using an IDE like PyCharm or VS Code, you can run your script by clicking a "Run" button.

For example, in VS Code:

1. Open your script (hello.py).
2. Click **Run > Start Debugging** or press F5.

For PyCharm:

1. Open your script.
2. Click **Run > Run 'hello.py'**.

This is a convenient way to run scripts without using the terminal.

You've now written and run your first Python program, understood the basics of syntax, and learned how to execute scripts from different environments. You're no longer just a spectator—you're officially a Python programmer!

In the next chapter, we'll dive deeper into Python syntax, variables, loops, and functions. But for now, take a moment to appreciate the power you've just unlocked.

Python is simple, yet incredibly powerful. And you're just getting started.

2

Chapter 2: Mastering Python Syntax and Basic Structures

Variables and Data Types

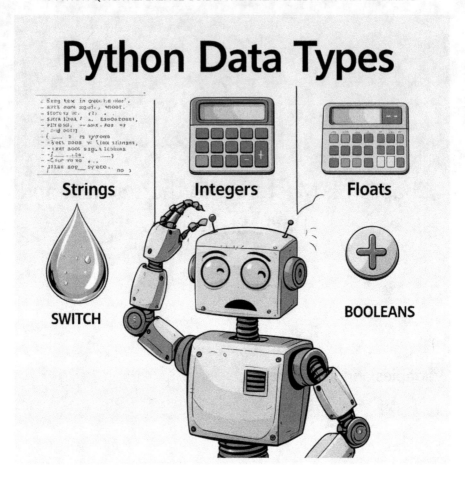

Defining Variables and Assigning Values

I n Python, variables are like magic boxes where you can store information. Unlike other languages that demand you to specify what type of data you want to store upfront, Python takes a more laid-back approach. You simply assign a value to a name, and Python figures out the rest. It's like hiring an assistant who just *knows* what you mean—no unnecessary questions asked.

Example:

```
name = "Alice" # A string (text)
   age = 30 # An integer (whole number)
   height = 5.7 # A float (decimal number)
   is_python_fun = True # A boolean (True/False)
```

Here's the kicker: You don't need to declare the type of a variable explicitly. Python dynamically assigns the type based on the value. If you later decide that age should be a string instead of a number, Python won't throw a tantrum—it will simply adapt.

```
   age = "thirty" # Python shrugs and goes with the flow
```

Variable Naming Rules

- Variable names **must** start with a letter or underscore (_), not a number.
- You **cannot** use Python's reserved keywords (e.g., if, def, class).
- Variable names **are case-sensitive** (so Age and age are different variables).
- Use descriptive names (user_age is better than x).

Common Data Types: Strings, Integers, Floats, and Booleans

Python has several built-in data types, but let's focus on the essentials:

Strings (str)

Strings are sequences of characters enclosed in quotes. Python doesn't discriminate—it accepts single ('), double ("), and even triple (''' or """) quotes.

```
   text = "Hello, World!"
   multiline_text = '''This is a
```

multiline string.''' # Triple quotes allow multiple lines

Integers (int)

Integers are whole numbers—positive, negative, or zero. They're great for counting, looping, and causing off-by-one errors.

```
score = 100
negative_number = -42
zero = 0
```


Floats (float)

Floats represent decimal numbers. They're essential when dealing with anything remotely scientific or financial (unless you enjoy losing pennies to rounding errors).

```
pi = 3.14159
price = 19.99
```


Booleans (bool)

Booleans hold only two values: True or False. They're the backbone of decision-making in Python.

```
is_daytime = True
is_hungry = False
```

Type Conversions and Type Checking

Sometimes, you need to convert data from one type to another. Python makes this easy with built-in functions.

Type Conversion (Casting)

- int() converts to an integer.
- float() converts to a float.
- str() converts to a string.
- bool() converts to a boolean.

```
num_str = "123"
    num_int = int(num_str) # Converts "123" to 123 (integer)
    num_float = float(num_int) # Converts 123 to 123.0 (float)
    num_bool = bool(num_int) # Converts 123 to True (boolean)
```

Be cautious when converting between types, though. Not all conversions make sense:

```
    int("hello") # This will raise a ValueError
```

Checking Data Types

If you ever wonder what type a variable is, Python has your back with the type() function:

```
    print(type(42)) # Output: <class 'int'>
    print(type("hello")) # Output: <class 'str'>
```

Pro Tip: Use isinstance()

If you want to check whether a variable belongs to a certain type, use isinstance():

```
print(isinstance(42, int)) # True
print(isinstance("Python", str)) # True
print(isinstance(3.14, float)) # True
```

Variables and data types in Python are incredibly flexible, making coding faster and more intuitive. Just remember:

1. Variables don't need explicit declarations.
2. Python figures out the data type for you.
3. You can convert between types when needed, but always check before doing so.

Now that you're armed with this knowledge, go forth and assign variables like a Python pro! 🐍

Control Flow (Conditionals and Loops) in Python

If Python were a grand stage play, **control flow** would be the director, ensuring that every actor (code block) delivers its lines at the right time. Without control flow, your program would execute straight through like a clueless intern reading from a script—no dramatic pauses, no decisions, just a mindless sprint to the finish. Fortunately, Python gives us tools like **if statements**, **loops**, and **loop control statements** to bring order and finesse to our programs.

1. Using if, else, and elif Statements

Think of an if statement as your program's ability to make decisions—like whether to order a coffee or a triple-shot espresso (because caffeine is life). The **if-else** structure allows your code to branch in different directions depending on conditions.

The Basic if Statement

Here's a simple example:

```
coffee = "hot"
if coffee == "hot":
print("Sip carefully, it's hot!")
```

Python checks if coffee is "hot". If true, it executes the print statement. Otherwise, it moves on as if nothing happened—like your email to customer support.

Adding an else Clause

But what if the coffee isn't hot? Enter the else clause:

```
coffee = "cold"
if coffee == "hot":
print("Sip carefully, it's hot!")
else:
print("Microwave it before drinking!")
```

Now your program can react to **both** hot and not-hot coffee situations. More realistic already!

The Versatile elif Clause

What if there are **multiple** possible scenarios? That's where elif (else-if) comes in:

```
temperature = 15
if temperature > 30:
print("It's boiling! Ice cream time!")
elif 20 <= temperature <= 30:
print("A nice sunny day!")
elif 10 <= temperature < 20:
print("A bit chilly, grab a sweater!")
else:
print("Freezing! Stay indoors!")
```

Python evaluates each condition in sequence. The moment it finds a **true** condition, it executes that block and **skips the rest**. Kind of like how we all skip Terms & Conditions agreements.

2. Writing for and while Loops

Loops are the bread and butter of programming. Instead of writing the same code **over and over**, loops let you automate repetition—because typing is overrated.

The for Loop: Iterating Like a Pro

A for loop lets you iterate over a sequence (like a list, tuple, or range) effortlessly:

```
fruits = ["apple", "banana", "cherry"]
for fruit in fruits:
print(f"I love {fruit}!")
```

Output:
  I love apple!
  I love banana!
  I love cherry!

The for loop picks one fruit at a time and runs the print function before moving to the next. Think of it as a conveyor belt, efficiently delivering items to your code.

Looping Through a Range

If you just need numbers, use range():

```
for i in range(5):
print(f"Iteration {i}")
```

This runs five times, with i taking values from **0 to 4** (because Python starts counting at zero like a toddler counting candy pieces).

The while Loop: Repeat Until Conditions Change

A while loop runs **as long as** a condition remains true.

```
count = 3
while count > 0:
print(f"Countdown: {count}")
count -= 1
print("Blast off!")
```

Output:
  Countdown: 3
  Countdown: 2
  Countdown: 1
  Blast off!

Be **careful** with while loops! If the condition never becomes false, your loop will **run forever**—like that one friend who won't stop talking.

3. Understanding Loop Control Statements (break, continue)

Sometimes, you need to exert **extra control** over your loops. Enter break and continue.

Breaking Out of a Loop (break)

break **stops** a loop early, like ghosting a bad date:

```
for number in range(1, 6):
if number == 3:
print("Stopping at 3!")
break
print(number)
```

Output:

```
1
2
Stopping at 3!
```

The moment number hits 3, the loop **terminates**.

Skipping an Iteration (continue)

continue **skips** an iteration and moves to the next one:

```
for number in range(1, 6):
if number == 3:
print("Skipping 3!")
continue
```

```
print(number)
```

Output:
```
1
2
Skipping 3!
4
5
```

When number is 3, continue skips the print(number) statement and goes straight to the next iteration.

Mastering **conditionals and loops** is like mastering the art of decision-making and repetition. You get to **control** your program's flow, ensuring it **reacts** to changes dynamically while avoiding unnecessary code duplication. Now go forth and **automate wisely**—because typing the same thing twice is just inefficient.

Defining and Calling Functions

Functions in Python

Ah, functions—the superheroes of Python programming. They are like the baristas at your favorite coffee shop: you tell them what you want (parameters), and they give you exactly what you asked for (return values). Without functions, your code would be a disorganized mess, much like a kitchen after a toddler's cooking experiment.

In Python, defining a function is as simple as using the def keyword:
```
def greet():
print("Hello, world!")
```

This function, greet(), doesn't take any parameters and simply prints a friendly message. Calling it is just as easy:

```
greet()
```

And voilà! You've just successfully summoned a function.

Function Parameters and Return Values

Functions become truly powerful when they accept parameters and return values. Think of parameters as ingredients you give to a chef—they dictate the final dish. Return values, on the other hand, are what you get after the chef works their magic.

Example:
```
def add(a, b):
return a + b
```

```
result = add(5, 3)
print(result) # Outputs: 8
```

Here, a and b are the ingredients, and the return statement is the final dish.

Scope and Lifetime of Variables (Local vs Global)

Scope in Python refers to where a variable can be accessed. It's like VIP access at a concert—some variables can go backstage (global scope), while others are stuck in general admission (local scope).

Example:
```
global_var = "I exist everywhere!"
```

```
def my_function():
local_var = "I exist only inside this function!"
print(local_var)
```

```
print(global_var) # Works fine
    my_function() # Works fine
    #print(local_var) # This would throw an error!
```

Global variables can be accessed from anywhere, but local variables only exist within the function they were created in. If you try to access a local variable outside its function, Python will give you an error faster than a cat knocking over a coffee mug.

Wrapping Up

Functions in Python are essential for keeping your code organized, reusable, and readable. By mastering parameters, return values, and scope, you're well on your way to writing clean and efficient Python code. Now, go forth and function like a pro!

3

Chapter 3: Working with Python Libraries and Data Structures

Python is like a Swiss Army knife—it comes packed with built-in tools (libraries) and handy compartments (data structures) to solve all sorts of problems. If you've ever wondered how Python can handle everything from managing your grocery list to performing complex data analysis, you're in the right place. In this chapter, we'll explore Python's key data structures and its powerful standard libraries. Strap in—this is where Python truly starts to shine!

Lists and Tuples in Python: Your Ultimate Guide to Data Management

If programming were a dinner party, lists and tuples would be the guests who always show up. They're essential, versatile, and incredibly useful for managing data in Python. But like any good party guests, they have distinct personalities: lists are flexible and mutable, while tuples are stubbornly immutable. Let's dive into the world of these fundamental Python data structures and see how they can make your life easier.

Creating and Modifying Lists

What is a List?

A list in Python is like a Swiss Army knife—capable of holding multiple values in a single variable. It's an ordered, mutable collection that can store elements of different data types. Need a mix of strings, integers, and even other lists? No problem—lists have you covered.

Creating a List

Defining a list in Python is as simple as putting values inside square brackets:

```
fruits = ["apple", "banana", "cherry"]
numbers = [1, 2, 3, 4, 5]
mixed_list = ["hello", 42, 3.14, True]
```

That's it—you now have lists that can store and organize data.

Modifying Lists

Since lists are mutable, we can change their content without breaking a sweat. Here's how you can modify lists:

1. Adding Elements

- Using append() to add an item at the end:fruits.append("orange")
- Using insert() to place an item at a specific position:fruits.insert(1, "mango")
- Using extend() to add multiple elements:fruits.extend(["grape", "pineapple"])

2. Removing Elements

- Using remove() to delete a specific element:fruits.remove("banana")
- Using pop() to remove an item by index:removed_item = fruits.pop(2)
- Using del to obliterate an item (or the entire list):del fruits[0] # Deletes the first item

del fruits # Deletes the entire list

3. Updating Elements

Since lists are mutable, changing a value is easy:
fruits[0] = "kiwi" # Replaces "apple" with "kiwi"

Accessing Elements, Slicing, and Iterating Over Lists

Accessing Elements

Lists are indexed, meaning every item has a position starting from 0. Accessing an element is as simple as:

```
print(fruits[1]) # Outputs 'banana'
```

You can also use negative indices to count from the end:

```
print(fruits[-1]) # Outputs the last item
```

Slicing Lists

Need only a portion of the list? Slicing helps:

```
print(fruits[1:3]) # Gets elements from index 1 to 2 (excluding 3)
print(fruits[:2]) # Gets the first two elements
print(fruits[2:]) # Gets elements from index 2 to the end
```

Iterating Over Lists

1. Using a for Loop

```
for fruit in fruits:
    print(fruit)
```

2. Using List Comprehension

```
uppercase_fruits = [fruit.upper() for fruit in fruits]
```

3. Using enumerate() to Get Index and Value

```
for index, fruit in enumerate(fruits):
    print(f"Index {index}: {fruit}")
```

Understanding Tuples and Their Immutability

What is a Tuple?

A tuple is like a list's unchangeable sibling. It's an ordered collection of elements, but once created, it cannot be modified (hence the immutability). Tuples are defined using parentheses:

```
coordinates = (10, 20)
colors = ("red", "green", "blue")
mixed_tuple = (1, "hello", 3.14)
```

Why Use Tuples?

1. **Performance**: Tuples are faster than lists.
2. **Safety**: Since tuples are immutable, they prevent accidental modification.
3. **Dictionary Keys**: Tuples can be used as dictionary keys, whereas lists cannot.

Accessing Elements in Tuples

Tuples use the same indexing and slicing as lists:

```
print(colors[1]) # Outputs 'green'
print(colors[:2]) # Outputs ('red', 'green')
```

Tuple Unpacking

Tuples allow easy variable unpacking:

```
x, y = coordinates
print(x) # Outputs 10
print(y) # Outputs 20
```

Converting Between Lists and Tuples

Need to convert a list to a tuple (or vice versa)? No problem:

```
list_from_tuple = list(colors)
tuple_from_list = tuple(fruits)
```

Lists and tuples are the bread and butter of Python's data management. Need flexibility? Use a list. Need something set in stone? Go with a tuple.

Dictionaries and Sets: The Dynamic Duo of Data Storage

Welcome to the wonderful world of **Dictionaries and Sets**, where data finds a cozy home in neatly labeled keys, and duplicate values get the boot faster than an uninvited guest at a VIP party. Whether you're storing user information, counting word frequencies, or just trying to keep track of your grocery list without repeating 'buy milk' three times, these two structures will save the day!

1. Using Dictionaries to Store Key-Value Pairs

What is a Dictionary?

A **dictionary** in Python is like a real-world dictionary, except instead of looking up words for definitions, you look up **keys** for their associated **values**. Think of it as the Swiss Army knife of data storage: flexible, efficient, and always ready for action.

Why Use a Dictionary?

- **Fast lookups**: No need to scan an entire list; just grab the value using the key.
- **Flexible storage**: Mix and match data types (strings, numbers, lists, even other dictionaries).
- **Readable and intuitive**: Makes data more structured and accessible.

Creating a Dictionary

The syntax is ridiculously simple:

```
# Creating a dictionary
user_info = {
"name": "Alice",
"age": 30,
"city": "New York"
}
print(user_info["name"]) # Output: Alice
```

Adding and Modifying Entries

```
user_info["email"] = "alice@example.com" # Adding a new key-value pair
    user_info["age"] = 31 # Updating an existing value
```

Deleting a Key-Value Pair

```
del user_info["city"] # Alice has moved!
```

Iterating Over a Dictionary

```
for key, value in user_info.items():
    print(f"{key}: {value}")
```

2. Set Operations and Properties

What is a Set?

A **set** is a collection of **unique** elements. If a dictionary is like a VIP guest list with assigned seats, a set is the list of people who actually showed up (no duplicates allowed!).

Why Use a Set?

- **Eliminates duplicates**: Perfect for filtering unique values.
- **Fast membership testing**: Checking if an item is in a set is faster than in a list.
- **Supports mathematical operations**: Union, intersection, and difference make data manipulation a breeze.

Creating a Set

```
# Creating a set
    unique_numbers = {1, 2, 3, 3, 4, 5}
    print(unique_numbers) # Output: {1, 2, 3, 4, 5}
```

Adding and Removing Elements

```
unique_numbers.add(6) # Add a new element
    unique_numbers.remove(3) # Remove an existing element
```

Set Operations

```
a = {1, 2, 3, 4}
    b = {3, 4, 5, 6}

print(a | b) # Union: {1, 2, 3, 4, 5, 6}
    print(a & b) # Intersection: {3, 4}
    print(a - b) # Difference: {1, 2}
    print(a ^ b) # Symmetric Difference: {1, 2, 5, 6}
```

3. Practical Examples of Dictionaries and Sets in Code

Example 1: Counting Word Frequencies with a Dictionary

Ever wanted to find out which words you overuse in your writing? Here's a quick way to count words in a text:

```
from collections import Counter
```

```
def word_count(text):
    words = text.split()
    return Counter(words)

text = "hello world hello python"
    print(word_count(text)) # Output: {'hello': 2, 'world': 1, 'python': 1}
```

Example 2: Removing Duplicates from a List with a Set

```
emails = ["a@example.com", "b@example.com", "a@example.com",
"c@example.com"]
    unique_emails = set(emails)
    print(unique_emails) # Output: {'a@example.com', 'b@example.com',
'c@example.com'}
```

Example 3: Finding Common Friends with Set Intersection

```
alice_friends = {"Bob", "Charlie", "David"}
    bob_friends = {"Alice", "Charlie", "Eve"}
    common_friends = alice_friends & bob_friends
    print(common_friends) # Output: {'Charlie'}
```

Dictionaries and sets may seem simple, but they are the **unsung heroes** of data handling in Python.

Using Built-in Libraries

Importing and Using Python's Standard Libraries

One of Python's biggest strengths is its vast collection of built-in libraries. Instead of reinventing the wheel (or rewriting functions that already exist), Python gives you ready-made tools for math, date handling, file operations, and much more. Let's dive into a few key libraries and how they can make your life easier.

The math Library: Because Counting on Fingers Doesn't Scale

Python's math library is your best friend for mathematical operations. From basic arithmetic to trigonometry, logarithms, and constants like π, it's got you covered.

```
import math
```

```
print(math.sqrt(16)) # Square root: 4.0
    print(math.pi) # Value of π
    print(math.sin(math.radians(90))) # Sine of 90 degrees
```

The datetime Library: Because "Monday" Isn't a Datatype

Handling dates and times can be painful, but Python's datetime module simplifies it.

```
from datetime import datetime
```

```
now = datetime.now()
    print("Current Date and Time:", now)
    print("Formatted Date:", now.strftime('%Y-%m-%d %H:%M:%S'))
```

Practical Examples of os, random, and sys Libraries

The os Library: Navigating Your File System Like a Pro

Python's os module lets you interact with your operating system—navigating directories, creating files, and more.

```
import os

print("Current Working Directory:", os.getcwd())
   os.mkdir("new_folder") # Creates a new directory
```

The random Library: Because Life is Full of Surprises

The random module is perfect for simulations, games, or just messing with your friends.

```
import random

print(random.randint(1, 100)) # Random integer between 1 and 100
   print(random.choice(['apple', 'banana', 'cherry'])) # Random selection
from a list
```

The sys Library: Talking Directly to Python's Brain

The sys module provides system-specific parameters and functions, such as accessing command-line arguments.

```
import sys

print("Python Version:", sys.version)
```

Understanding the Importance of Python Packages

Python's ecosystem is powered by thousands of open-source packages, accessible via pip (Python's package manager). Whether you need data analysis (pandas), web scraping (BeautifulSoup), or machine learning (scikit-learn), there's a package for you.

pip install requests # Install the requests library for handling HTTP requests

By using built-in and third-party libraries, Python allows you to work efficiently, reduce redundancy, and write clean, maintainable code. Now, go forth and import like a champion!

4

Chapter 4: Advanced Python Concepts and Productivity Tips

C ongratulations! You've made it through the basics, survived control flow, and wrangled Python's built-in libraries like a true coder. Now, it's time to level up. This chapter dives into advanced Python concepts and powerful productivity tips that will make your code cleaner, your debugging smoother, and your Python skills sharper than a fresh pair of parentheses.

Working with Files

Reading from and Writing to Files

Ah, files—the digital scrolls of our age. Whether you're storing precious data or just making a text file to hold your shopping list, Python makes file handling surprisingly easy. Let's start by cracking open a file and seeing what's inside.

Reading a File

Python's open() function is your go-to tool for reading files. By default, it opens files in read mode ('r'). Let's see it in action:

```
with open('example.txt', 'r') as file:
content = file.read()
print(content)
```

Boom! Just like that, Python reads the entire file into a variable. But what if your file is 10GB of cat memes? Reading it all at once isn't a great idea. Instead, read it line by line:

```
with open('example.txt', 'r') as file:
for line in file:
print(line.strip())
```

Writing to a File

Creating and writing to a file follows the same pattern, except now we use 'w' mode:

```
with open('example.txt', 'w') as file:
file.write("Hello, world!\n")
```

Remember: Writing in 'w' mode **overwrites** the file. If you want to add to an existing file, use 'a' (append mode):

```
with open('example.txt', 'a') as file:
file.write("Appending this line!\n")
```

File Handling and Error Management (try-except Blocks)

Files are like toddlers—they can be unpredictable. A file might not exist, permissions could be wrong, or your computer could spontaneously combust (okay, maybe not). That's why we handle errors gracefully using try-except:

```
try:
with open('non_existent_file.txt', 'r') as file:
content = file.read()
except FileNotFoundError:
print("Oops! The file doesn't exist.")
except PermissionError:
print("You don't have permission to access this file.")
except Exception as e:
print(f"Something went wrong: {e}")
```

Managing File Paths and Directories with os

Python's os module lets you navigate the file system like a digital ninja. Want to check if a file exists?

```
import os
```

```
if os.path.exists('example.txt'):
print("File exists!")
else:
print("No such file.")
```

Need to list all files in a directory?

```
print(os.listdir('.')) # Lists files in the current directory
```

Want to make a new folder?

```
os.mkdir('new_folder')
```

And if you need to move or delete files, Python's shutil module is your best friend:

```
import shutil
```

```
shutil.move('example.txt', 'new_folder/example.txt') # Move file
    shutil.rmtree('new_folder') # Delete folder and contents
```

Wrapping Up

Working with files is an essential skill in Python, whether you're saving user data, logging errors, or hoarding cat memes. With the open() function, try-except blocks, and the mighty os module, you're now equipped to conquer file management like a pro.

Reading from and Writing to Files

Python makes working with files a breeze. Here's a quick example of how to open a file, read its contents, and close it properly:

```
with open('example.txt', 'r') as file:
content = file.read()
print(content)
```

Want to write something? Easy:

```
with open('example.txt', 'w') as file:
file.write("Hello, Python world!")
```

File Handling and Error Management (try-except Blocks)

Because things go wrong in programming (and life), handling errors is key. Using try-except ensures your program doesn't crash and burn when a file goes missing:

```
try:
with open('non_existent_file.txt', 'r') as file:
content = file.read()
except FileNotFoundError:
print("Oops! The file doesn't exist.")
```

Managing File Paths and Directories with os

Navigating file paths like a ninja:

```
import os
print(os.getcwd()) # Prints current working directory
os.mkdir('new_directory') # Creates a new folder
```

Error Handling and Debugging

Understanding Different Error Types in Python

Python throws a tantrum (raises an exception) when something goes wrong. Some common ones:

- SyntaxError: You broke Python's grammar rules.
- TypeError: You mixed up data types.
- NameError: You used a variable that doesn't exist.

· IndexError: You tried to access an out-of-bounds index.

Using try, except, else, and finally

Python lets you try things out, catch errors, and even execute cleanup code:

```
try:
num = int("Oops") # This will cause a ValueError
except ValueError:
print("That's not a valid number!")
else:
print("Conversion successful!")
finally:
print("Execution complete!")
```

Debugging Code with Print Statements and Python's Built-in Debugger

Debugging is an art. The simple way:

```
x = 10
y = 0
print(f"x: {x}, y: {y}") # Spot the issue before division
print(x / y) # Oops! ZeroDivisionError
```

Or use Python's built-in debugger:

```
import pdb
pdb.set_trace()
```

Now you can step through your code like Sherlock Holmes!

That wraps up this section! Debug wisely, and remember: Errors are just Python's way of keeping you humble.

Error Handling and Debugging

- Understanding different error types in Python
- Using try, except, else, and finally
- Debugging code with print statements and Python's built-in debugger

Python Productivity Tips

Code Optimization Techniques

Writing efficient Python code is like packing a suitcase—if you don't do it right, you'll be stuck with unnecessary baggage. Optimizing your code can make it run faster and use fewer resources. Here are some battle-tested techniques:

List Comprehensions Over Loops: Instead of writing a long for loop, use list comprehensions. They are faster and more Pythonic.

squares = [x**2 for x in range(10)] # Faster than using a loop

- **Use Generators for Large Data Processing**: Instead of storing all data in memory, use generators to yield values lazily.def large_data_stream():

for i in range(10**6):
    yield i

- **Built-in Functions are Your Friends**: Python has tons of built-in functions that are optimized in C. Use them instead of reinventing the wheel.sum(range(1000)) # Faster than looping through manually

- **Writing Clean, Pythonic Code**

Writing Pythonic code means following best practices that make your code readable, maintainable, and elegant. Here's how to make your code beautiful:

- **Follow PEP 8**: Python's official style guide ensures consistency. Stick to it unless you have a really, really good reason not to.
- **Use Meaningful Variable Names**: x = 10 is fine in math class, but user_age = 10 makes more sense in code.

Avoid Unnecessary Nesting: Deeply nested loops and conditionals make your code harder to read. Use early returns instead.

```
def is_valid_age(age):
if age < 18:
return False
return True
```

Introduction to Common Python Libraries for Productivity

Python's rich ecosystem of libraries can help you do more with less effort. Here are some must-know libraries:

pandas: A powerhouse for data manipulation. Read CSVs, filter data, and do powerful analysis in just a few lines.

```
import pandas as pd
df = pd.read_csv("data.csv")
print(df.head())
```

- **numpy**: Essential for numerical computing. Use it to perform fast array operations.import numpy as np

```
arr = np.array([1, 2, 3])
print(arr.mean())
```

- **requests**: The best way to make HTTP requests in Python.import requests

```
response = requests.get("https://api.github.com")
  print(response.json())
```

These libraries supercharge your Python experience and help you get things done quickly and efficiently.

5

Wrapping Up Your Python Journey

C ongratulations! You've made it through the ins and outs of Python, from humble print statements to advanced productivity tips. By now, you should feel like a Python pro—at least enough to impress your colleagues, debug like a champ, and automate tasks you never thought possible.

But before you ride off into the sunset with your newfound Python mastery, let's take a moment to reflect on what we've covered, why it matters, and where you can go next.

The Road You've Traveled

Over the past chapters, you've navigated the winding roads of Python's syntax, libraries, and best practices. Let's quickly recap the highlights:

- **Chapter 1: Getting Started with Python** – You learned what Python is, why it's a favorite among developers, how to set it up, and how to run your first Python script.
- **Chapter 2: Mastering Python Syntax and Basic Structures** – We dove deep into variables, data types, conditionals, loops, and functions. In short, the fundamental building blocks of every Python program.
- **Chapter 3: Working with Python Libraries and Data Structures** – You explored lists, tuples, dictionaries, and sets, along with some of Python's most powerful built-in libraries.
- **Chapter 4: Advanced Python Concepts and Productivity Tips** – We covered error handling, debugging, working with files, and optimizing your Python code for peak efficiency.

At this point, you've essentially built yourself a Python survival toolkit. Whether you want to analyze data, automate tasks, or even develop web applications, you have the foundational knowledge to get started.

Why Python Matters

So, why did you just spend all this time learning Python? Here's why:

- **Versatility** – Python is used everywhere—from web development and data science to AI and automation.
- **Readability** – With its clean and simple syntax, Python makes coding more intuitive and enjoyable.
- **Community & Libraries** – With a vast ecosystem of libraries and an active developer community, you'll never feel alone on your coding journey.

- **Career Growth** – Python skills are highly sought after, making it an excellent addition to your professional toolkit.

Whether you're a beginner or a seasoned programmer looking to refine your skills, Python is the language that keeps on giving.

Where to Go Next?

So, what's next on your Python journey? Here are some paths you might consider:

1. Dive into Real-World Projects

Theory is great, but practice is where the magic happens. Try building:

- A web scraper to automate data collection
- A simple chatbot
- A personal finance tracker
- A Python-based game using Pygame

2. Explore Specialized Fields

Python is used across multiple industries. Depending on your interests, you can explore:

- **Data Science & Machine Learning** – Learn Pandas, NumPy, Scikit-learn, and TensorFlow.
- **Web Development** – Get hands-on with Flask or Django.
- **Automation & Scripting** – Use Python to automate daily tasks and improve productivity.
- **Cybersecurity & Ethical Hacking** – Learn how Python is used in security testing.

3. Join the Python Community

The Python community is one of the most welcoming out there. Engage by:

- Participating in online forums (Reddit, Stack Overflow, Dev.to)
- Contributing to open-source projects on GitHub
- Attending local Python meetups or virtual hackathons

4. Never Stop Learning

Python is constantly evolving. Stay up to date by:

- Following Python-related blogs and YouTube channels
- Reading official documentation and tutorials
- Experimenting with new libraries and frameworks

Parting Words of Wisdom

Python is more than just a programming language—it's a gateway to problem-solving, creativity, and innovation. Whether you're automating tasks, analyzing data, or developing the next big application, Python is there to make your life easier and your work more efficient.

As you continue your Python journey, keep this in mind:

- **Don't be afraid to break things.** Debugging is part of the learning process.
- **Write clean, readable code.** Your future self (and your colleagues) will thank you.
- **Stay curious and keep experimenting.** The best way to master Python is by building and breaking things repeatedly.

With that, I leave you with one final challenge—go forth and code something amazing!

6

References

Chun, W. J. (2012). *Core Python Programming* (2nd ed.). Prentice Hall.

Guido van Rossum, & Python Software Foundation. (2023). *The Python Language Reference, Release 3.11.5.* Python Software Foundation. Retrieved from https://docs.python.org/3/reference/

Harris, C. R., Millman, K. J., van der Walt, S. J., Gommers, R., Virtanen, P., Cournapeau, D., ... & Oliphant, T. E. (2020). *Array programming with NumPy.* Nature, 585(7825), 357-362. doi:10.1038/s41586-020-2649-2

Pilgrim, M. (2004). *Dive into Python.* Apress.

Smith, A. (2024, August 31). *I learned the language of computer programming in my 50s – here's what I discovered.* The Guardian. Retrieved from https://www.theguardian.com/technology/article/2024/aug/31/learning-computer-programming-language-coding

W3Schools. (2024). *Python Reference Documentation.* W3Schools. Retrieved from https://www.w3schools.com/python/python_reference.asp

Wikipedia Contributors. (2024). *Python (programming language).* Wikipedia, The Free Encyclopedia. Retrieved from https://en.wikipedia.org/wiki/Python_(programming_language)

Wikipedia Contributors. (2024). *Zen of Python.* Wikipedia, The Free Encyclopedia. Retrieved from https://en.wikipedia.org/wiki/Zen_of_Python

7

About the Author: Jordan Loopman

J ordan Loopman is a seasoned software engineer, technical educator, and Python enthusiast with a passion for simplifying complex programming concepts. With over a decade of experience in software development, he has worked across various industries, including fintech, data science, and automation. His ability to distill intricate coding principles into practical, easy-to-understand techniques has made him a go-to expert for developers and tech enthusiasts alike.

Jordan's journey with Python began with a simple automation script, sparking an enduring fascination with the language's simplicity and power. He has since contributed to open-source projects, conducted training sessions for aspiring programmers, and developed countless tools to enhance productivity in the tech world.

When he's not coding or writing, Jordan enjoys exploring the latest advancements in AI, mentoring young developers, and brewing the perfect cup of coffee. His book, *Python Quick Reference Guide: The Cheat Sheet for Fast Learning*, serves as an essential companion for those looking to master Python efficiently and effectively.

II

A Small Request (But a Big Deal for Me!)

Hey, fellow Pythonista!

If you've made it this far, congratulations! You've leveled up your Python skills and survived my humor. Now, I have a simple favor to ask—leave a review!

Reviews help fellow programmers (and those still wondering if they should learn Python or take up underwater basket weaving instead) decide if this book is worth their time.

So, if you laughed at least once, learned something new, or just enjoyed my witty charm, please drop a review. If you didn't like it... well, pretend this page doesn't exist and go write some Python instead.

Happy coding, and may all your bugs be features!